Supporting Learning in Schools

Hampshire
County Council

Written by Tom Br

Illustrated by Nichol

H005108608

Schools Library Service

D1422338

Chapter 1

The cave was dark as Simon and Dan squeezed through the narrow passage. Cold water dripped on them from above and the air smelt of mould.

The only light came from the weak torches strapped to their foreheads. They came out into a big chamber and gathered round the tour guide. "This is the most famous painting in the caves," said the guide, pointing at a huge picture on the wall. "The Great Bull!"

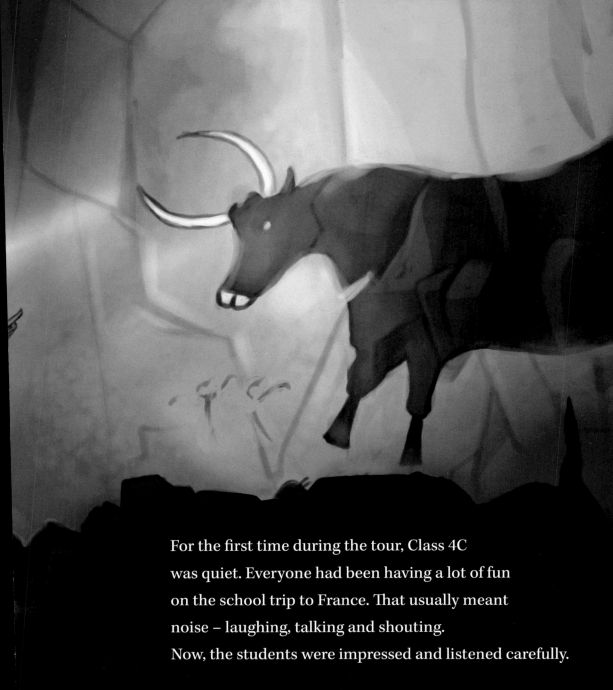

For the first time during the tour, Class 4C
was quiet. Everyone had been having a lot of fun
on the school trip to France. That usually meant
noise – laughing, talking and shouting.
Now, the students were impressed and listened carefully.

"This is the Hall of the Bulls," the guide told them. "These paintings are over 17,000 years old."

"That's nearly as old as Mr Archer," Simon whispered to Dan.

"I heard that," grumbled Mr Archer, their teacher. He was a big man and looked a bit like a bull himself.

"They're so old," the guide continued, "that some are very faded. No one knows what they are."

She pointed at some very faint marks in front of the bull.

"They could be birds," said Simon. "Those lines look like wings."

"They look like two monkeys to me," said Dan, "talking to the bull."

The tour was finished now and everyone else followed the guide outside.

"Come on," said Mr Archer. "If you don't hurry, we'll miss lunch."

"We're not hungry, sir," answered Dan. "We had a big breakfast."

"I am," grumbled Mr Archer. "Teachers get hungry too."

Mr Archer left the cave, but the boys were still looking at the paintings.

As they started to follow the rest of the class, they didn't see the rock
the other children had stepped over.
Dan tripped and grabbed Simon.
Suddenly, the cave started to shake
and they both crashed
to the ground.

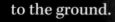

After a moment, the shaking stopped.

"What just happened?" Simon said, rubbing his head.

Dan sat up and looked around the cave, puzzled. "Maybe it was an earthquake? Where is everybody?"

Chapter 2

"That's strange, the paintings look clearer ..." Simon said, frowning, "but where's the painting of the Great Bull?" That part of the cave wall was blank.

"I dunno. Let's get out of here," said Dan. The pictures looked as though they had just been painted, not thousands of years old. The colours were bright and strong, and the bulls loomed out of the darkness at them. The cave suddenly felt cold and spooky.

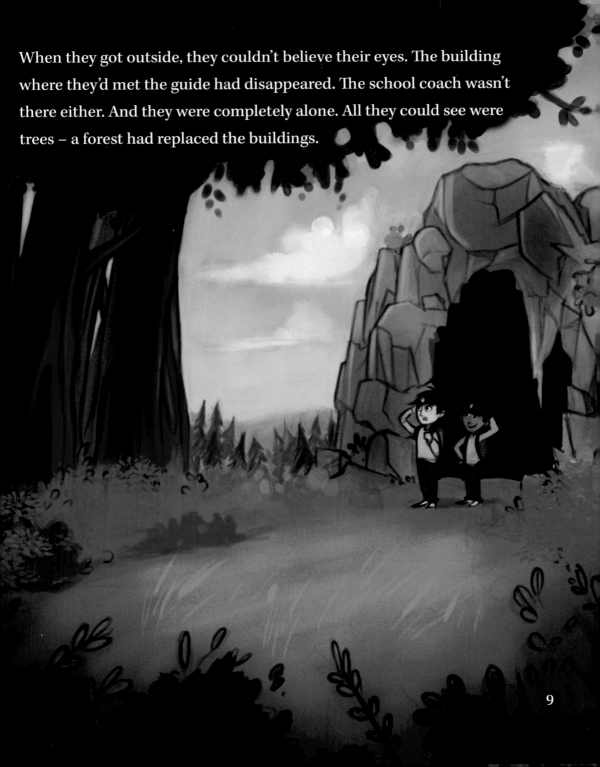

When they got outside, they couldn't believe their eyes. The building where they'd met the guide had disappeared. The school coach wasn't there either. And they were completely alone. All they could see were trees – a forest had replaced the buildings.

"Hello!" yelled Simon. "Anyone there?"

"What ..." whispered Dan, "... what happened to the buildings?"

The boys walked towards a line of smoke rising above the trees and found some people sitting around a fire, wearing strange clothes, fur and bits of leather.

"Let's say hello," said Dan. "They might know what happened."

As the boys walked over, two men jumped up. They ran towards the boys, grunting angrily.

"They don't look friendly," hissed Simon.

"But they might know what's happened to everyone," Dan said.
"Just smile!"

When the men got closer, Simon tried to smile. "Hi! I'm Simon,
and this is my friend Dan. Do you speak English? French?"

One of them reached out and poked Dan's backpack. He gave a grunt.

Dan looked at Simon. "I think that's a 'no'."

"Do you know where the buildings are?" Simon said very slowly.

The men just stared at them and frowned.

Dan stepped back. "Get ready to run; I think we're in trouble!"

"Wait! Let me try something," said Simon.

He pulled his lunchbox out of his backpack. The men looked confused. Simon slowly opened the lid and held up a sandwich. The cavemen made an "Ooh" noise. Simon took a bite and smiled, rubbing his stomach to show them how good it was.

One of the cavemen came forward and Simon gave him the sandwich. The man nibbled a tiny bit. He thought for a moment, then he smiled and shoved the rest of it into his mouth.

Simon laughed nervously. "You'd think they'd never seen a sandwich before!"

Dan suddenly looked a bit green. "Er, Simon? I don't think they *have* ever seen a sandwich before."

Simon looked at Dan. "What do you mean?"

"Well, they only speak 'grunt', they keep poking at your lunchbox and look at what they're wearing. I think we must've travelled back in time!"

"So these are *real* cavemen?" Simon gulped. "That's why all the buildings have gone! What do we do now?"

Dan thought for a moment. "I guess we try to make friends and then work out how to get back to *our* time."

A couple of cavemen kids came over and grunted at Simon and Dan.

"Er, I think that means 'hi'!" laughed Dan. He gave one of them a banana.

"You think these guys painted the caves?" Simon said. Dan just nodded.

"Then maybe they can help us get back to our time."

Simon and Dan started pointing back towards the caves.

At first, the cavemen kids didn't seem to understand. Then one of them nodded and grunted at Simon and Dan to follow her.

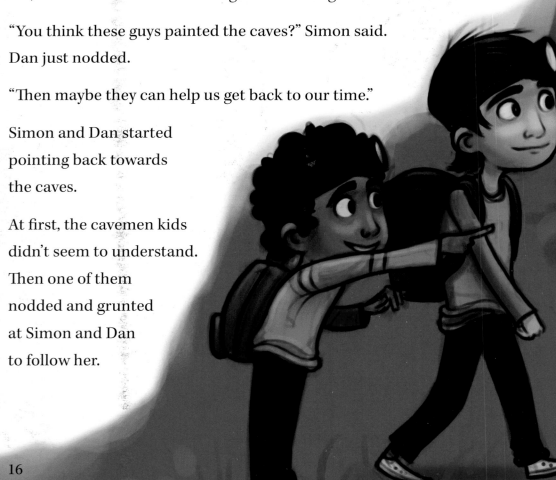

As they got nearer the caves, there was a great roaring sound and everyone stopped. Dan clutched at Simon's arm. There was something very big moving through the trees ahead.

Soon, they knew where the noise had come from. A giant bull was standing in front of the cave and it looked angry.

"Is that what I think it is?" asked Simon in a small voice. "How are we going to get past that thing?"

"Carefully," said Dan. "If we can't get back into the cave, we might be stuck here forever!"

The cavemen kids scrambled up the trees, waving urgently at Simon and Dan to copy them.

But Simon and Dan weren't fast enough. The bull made a deep grumbling noise and stared at them, breathing heavily through its nose.

Then it roared and charged at them. Its hooves sounded like thunder as they hit the ground. The boys ran back into the trees as fast as they could. The animal only stopped when it couldn't see them anymore.

"What ... now ...?" panted Simon, getting his breath back.

"Did you see? It looked like Mr Archer," wheezed Dan. "Shame it couldn't understand us like Mr Archer."

"Yeah," Simon said thoughtfully. "Hey, I've got an idea!"

He took his lunchbox out of his backpack and held it up.

"Teachers get hungry, too," Dan said, smiling.

Simon got a sandwich and threw it towards the animal. The bull moved away from the cave entrance and lumbered over to sniff at the bread.

Dan then threw it an apple. While the bull was greedily eating the food, the boys carefully walked round and back into the cave.

"That wasn't too difficult," said Dan.
"Now we can go home."

"Yeah," said Simon.
"But how?"

Now that they were in the cave, they didn't know what to do. There was no door with "future" or "home" written on it. They walked up and down, but they couldn't find a way back.

"Are we going to be here forever?" asked Dan.

"I hope not," said Simon.

The cavemen kids soon followed them inside. They pointed at Simon and Dan's torches and Dan showed them how to switch the light on and off.

Simon pointed at the paintings and then at the cavemen kids. "Did you paint these?" he asked.

The boy nodded. He went to the corner of the cave and carried over some sticky, coloured mud in his hand. Using his fingers, he showed Simon and Dan how they painted on the walls. The boy started to paint a big bull.

"Hey, that's the Great Bull we saw on the wall. The one with the monkeys," Dan said. "He must be copying the bull we just saw outside."

Next to the bull, the boy was painting two figures.

"Let me see," Simon said. He stepped forward, "Look at this! They look just like —"

As Simon moved closer, he tripped over the rock in the cave. Suddenly, the cave went black. Simon grabbed Dan's arm and the boys landed on the ground, banging their heads together.

When they looked up, Mr Archer was standing near the entrance to the cave. The cavemen kids were gone. The two boys were back in the future.

"Hurry up, you two," Mr Archer said. "I thought you were right behind me."

Simon and Dan looked at each other in amazement. They had been away for ages, but it must have only been minutes in their own time.

Dan was looking over at the painting of the bull. "Hey, Simon," he whispered. "I think I know what those lines in front of the bull are."

As they followed Mr Archer out of the cave, they took one last look at the painting. The faint lines looked like two boys. And they were feeding the bull.

Linking the present to the past

present

past

31

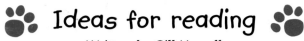

Ideas for reading

Written by Gill Howell
Primary Literacy Consultant

Learning objectives: (*word reading objectives correspond with White band; all other objectives correspond with Copper band*) continue to apply phonic knowledge and skills as the route to decode words until automatic decoding has become embedded and reading is fluent; drawing inferences such as inferring characters' feelings, thoughts and motives from their actions, and justifying inferences with evidence; predicting what might happen from details stated and implied

Curriculum links: History, Art

Interest words: prehistoric, mould, earthquake, thousands, building, leather, confused, stomach, nervously, urgently, creature, future

Word count: 1,537

Resources: paper, pens, collage materials, whiteboard, internet

Getting started

- Look at the cover and read the title together. Ask the children to describe what the illustration shows, then to predict what the Hall of the Bulls might be. Check that they recognise the head torches and ask them to suggest where the two children are and why torches are needed. Discuss the bull in the image. Ask them what it shows and who they think might have drawn it, and when.

- Turn to the back cover and read the blurb. Point out the word *prehistoric*. Ask them to read the word without the prefix *pre* and discuss the meaning of the prefix. Ask the children if they know what prehistoric means and explain as needed.

Reading and responding

- Ask the children to read the story together. Remind them to use their knowledge of phonics and the context of the sentences to help them work out new words, e.g. *famous* on p2.

- Pause on p5 when the marks are spotted near the bull. Ask the children to predict what they might be.